PUZZLE BOOK

DEADLY

CREATURES

FACT-PACKED FUN

Published by Collins
An imprint of HarperCollins Publishers
Westerhill Road
Bishopbriggs
Glasgow G64 2QT
www.harpercollins.co.uk

HarperCollins Publishers
1st Floor, Watermarque Building, Ringsend Road, Dublin 4, Ireland

In association with National Geographic Partners, LLC

NATIONAL GEOGRAPHIC and the Yellow Border Design are trademarks of the
National Geographic Society, used under license.

First published 2021

ISBN 978-0-00-843051-1

10 9 8 7 6 5 4 3 2 1

The contents of this publication are believed correct at the time of printing.
Nevertheless the publisher can accept no responsibility for errors or omissions,
changes in the detail given or for any expense or loss thereby caused.

HarperCollins does not warrant that any website mentioned in this title will be
provided uninterrupted, that any website will be error free, that defects will
be corrected, or that the website or the server that makes it available are free
of viruses or bugs. For full terms and conditions please refer to the site terms
provided on the website.

A catalogue record for this book is available from the British Library.

Printed in China by RR Donnelley APS Co Ltd.

If you would like to comment on any aspect of this book,
please contact us at the above address or online.
natgeokidsbooks.co.uk
collins.reference@harpercollins.co.uk

Paper from responsible sources.

Acknowledgements

Cover images © Shutterstock.com

P13 Dubois Sea Snake Donovan Klein/Alamy Stock Photo
All other images © Shutterstock.com

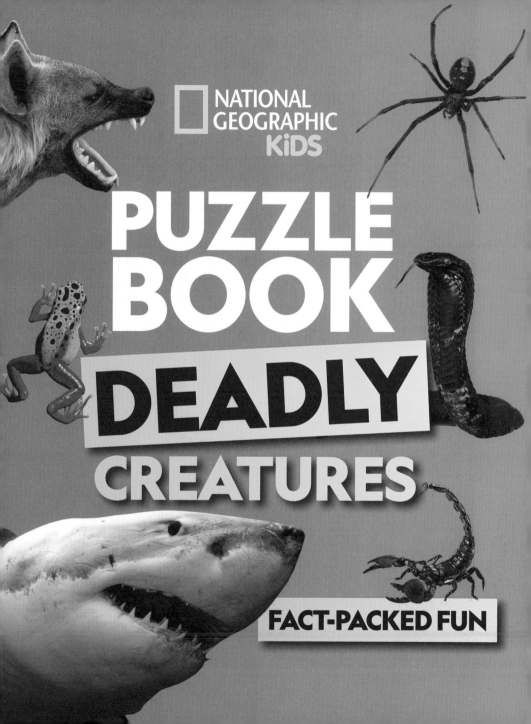

CONTENTS

UNDER THE SEA 6

IN THE AIR 24

IN THE JUNGLE 42

OVER THE SAVANNA 58

ACROSS THE DESERT 76

SOLUTIONS 94

UNDER THE SEA

How many creepy but incredible creatures lurk
beneath the water? Let's find out!
Dive into these fascinating facts and
puzzles all about the most deadly of
marine menaces...

GREAT WHITE SHARKS are known for their enormous size and killer bite. What is less well-known is that they are one of the longest-living shark species as they live for up to 70 years!

Crosswords

Help the sea creatures crack the crosswords by solving the clues below. Answers have the same amount of letters as the number in brackets. Can you work out the name of the underwater creatures using the letters in the shaded squares? See if you are right by flicking to page 94.

BEAKED SEA SNAKES contain enough venom to kill six adults!

Across

4 Leave a place (6)
6 Part of the foot of a horse (4)
7 Prison (4)
8 Underground plant part (4)
9 Limbs we walk on (4)
10 Steady; firmly fixed (6)

Down

1 Constant; lasting indefinitely (9)
2 Not giving enough attention to a task (8)
3 Animal with sharp teeth and a long tail (9)
5 Day before Friday (8)

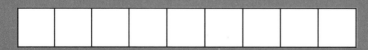

Across

4 Four-wheeled road vehicle (3)
6 Product used to clean hair (7)
7 Admiration for someone (7)
8 Bird kept on farms (7)
10 ___ instrument; e.g. trumpet or recorder (7)
11 Hint (3)

Down

1 Person who goes into space (9)
2 Fathers (4)
3 Quickest (9)
4 Item of clothing worn outside (4)
5 Shape with four straight sides (9)
8 Sleep in a tent (4)
9 Hit with the foot (4)

(3,5)

Sudokus

Help the bull shark solve the sudokus. Fill in the blank squares so that numbers 1 to 6 appear once in each row, column and 3 x 2 box. See if you are right by flicking to page 94.

BULL SHARKS are famously aggressive and have been known to attack hippos in African river deltas!

					2
4	5		1		
3	6				
				1	3
		6		2	4
2					

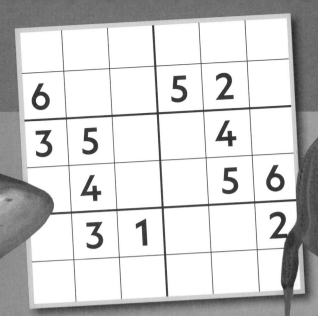

BOX JELLYFISH have 24 eyes in four clusters of six, they can chase down prey, and they have over 5,000 stinging cells on each tentacle!

Wordsearches

This great white shark is on the hunt for other deadly sea creatures. Can you help? Search left to right, up and down to find the creatures listed in the boxes below. See if you are right by flicking to page 94.

GREAT WHITES have up to 300 serrated teeth across several rows. Their exceptional sense of smell helps them detect and hunt for prey.

barracuda
great white
lionfish
needlefish
sea snake
squid
surgeonfish
tiger shark

j	g	r	e	a	t	w	h	i	t	e	u
a	s	e	z	z	p	s	n	t	s	b	q
n	e	f	z	k	r	u	i	q	c	a	x
e	j	t	i	g	e	r	s	h	a	r	k
e	s	l	t	s	d	g	p	s	n	r	p
d	t	i	r	e	t	e	r	r	k	a	o
l	y	o	o	a	r	o	s	c	t	c	i
e	l	n	o	s	w	n	q	r	y	u	t
f	m	f	e	n	u	f	u	o	t	d	y
i	l	i	a	a	z	i	i	g	u	a	i
s	o	s	l	k	x	s	d	v	x	p	u
h	u	h	s	e	s	h	a	w	m	o	f

```
k p w i l x b n g v z c
y t a u m m u j u i v s
c p e p c o l t y p p t
o a x a q r l k t e o o
n z f a j a s z t r c n
e w l o h y h c f f j e
s h q i o e a g e i t f
n p u f f e r f i s h i
a u u h s l k t r h k s
i a t i g e r f i s h h
l a i o f j r w r d x r
t r q c a n d i r u x s
```

bull shark
candiru
cone snail
moray eel
puffer fish
stonefish
tiger fish
viperfish

DUBOIS SEA SNAKES aren't just the most venomous sea snakes in the ocean, they're also some of the most venomous snakes in the world!

Mazes

Avoid the needlefish by swimming around
the maze until you reach the exit. See if
you are right by flicking to page 95.

NEEDLEFISH
can jump out of the
water at speeds of
60 km/h, which is
extremely dangerous if
something happens to be in
their way, because their
heads are shaped like
long sharp
needles!

HUMBOLDT SQUID have tentacles with razor-sharp grips in them and they are even known to eat each other when there is nothing to hunt! It's no wonder they're known as the 'red devils' of the ocean!

Spot the difference

Compare the lionfish images below.
Can you spot the five differences between the images?
See if you are right by flicking to page 95.

RED LIONFISH have a wild mane which is made up of venomous spines.

Guess what?

1. On average, how long do great white sharks live?
   a. 7 years
   b. 70 years
   c. 700 years

2. A blue-ringed octopus carries enough venom to kill how many people?
   a. 26
   b. 260
   c. 2,600

3. What is the most toxic animal on Earth?
   a. Burmese python
   b. Bluefin tuna
   c. Box jellyfish

4. Red lionfish have a wild mane of:
   a. Red hair
   b. Sharp teeth
   c. Venomous spines

5. What shark uses its wide head to trap and pin stingrays to the seafloor?
   a. Tiger shark
   b. Hammerhead shark
   c. Whale shark

6. In which ocean layer would you find the viperfish?
   a. Twilight zone
   b. Midnight zone
   c. Sunlight zone

7. Which feared fish use two sets of jaws to catch and kill their prey?
   a. Moray eels
   b. Clown fish
   c. Swordfish

8. Needlefish can jump out of the water at speeds of:
   a. 20 km/h
   b. 60 km/h
   c. 100 km/h

9. Which toxic fish is considered a delicacy in Japan?
   a. Pufferfish
   b. Salmon
   c. Sea bass

10. Beaked sea snakes grow to an average length of:
    a. 60 cm
    b. 120 cm
    c. 200 cm

STRIPED SURGEONFISH may look beautiful but they have scalpel-sharp spines near their tail fins.

Can you guess the answers to the deadly
sea animal questions?
Check your answers by flicking to page 95.

STONEFISH
are the most
venomous known fish
in the ocean. They have
13 spines on their backs,
each loaded with
deadly venom sacs!

Close-ups

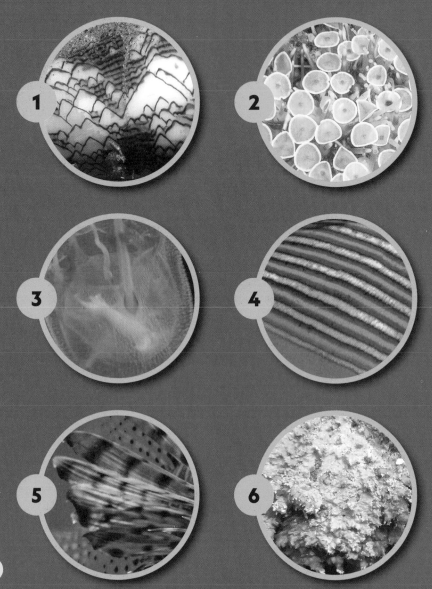

Can you match the beautiful but deadly close-ups on the left with the pictures below? See if you are right by flicking to page 95.

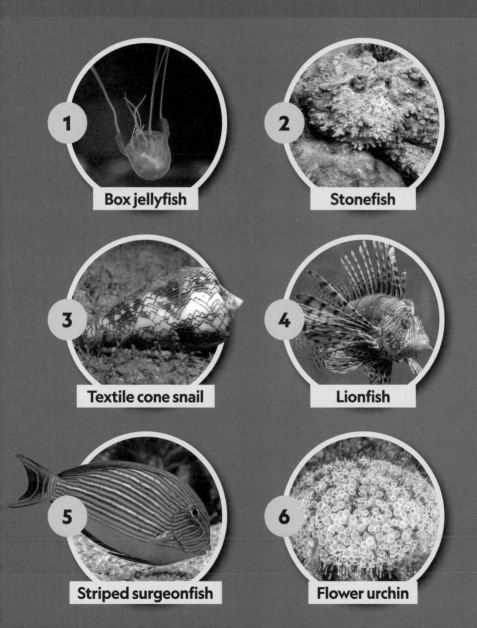

1 Box jellyfish

2 Stonefish

3 Textile cone snail

4 Lionfish

5 Striped surgeonfish

6 Flower urchin

Word jumbles

Rearrange the jumbled letters to form deadly marine species.
See if you are right by flicking to page 95.

R T G A E W T E H I

A E S K E A S N

F P S I H U F F E R

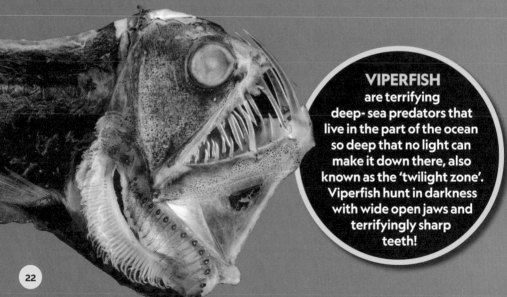

VIPERFISH
are terrifying
deep-sea predators that
live in the part of the ocean
so deep that no light can
make it down there, also
known as the 'twilight zone'.
Viperfish hunt in darkness
with wide open jaws and
terrifyingly sharp
teeth!

Word wheels

Can you spell the names of deadly sea creatures using all of the letters in each word wheel?
See if you are right by flicking to page 95.

TEXTILE CONE SNAILS are predatory sea snails; there is no known anti-venom available to cure the effects of their deadly venom. They have wonderful interlocking triangle patterns on their shells but make sure you admire them from far away!

IN THE AIR

Get ready for some perplexing puzzles and fatal facts about the deadliest winged creatures on the planet!

HONEYBEES are helpful because they pollinate plants but they can also be deadly! Around 1 in 4,000 humans are severely allergic to their venom.

Crosswords

Help the birds crack the crosswords by solving the clues below. Answers have the same amount of letters as the number in brackets. Can you work out the name of the winged creatures using the letters in the shaded squares? See if you are right by flicking to page 96.

CROWNED EAGLES
are impressive and powerful birds that have been known to eat monkeys!

Across
1. Object worn on a finger (4)
3. Furniture item you sit on (4)
5. ___ Day: 25th December (9)
6. A company that issues books for sale (9)
8. The same as something else (9)
10. Small amphibian you might find in a pond (4)
11. Hot molten rock from a volcano (4)

Down
1. Hotel area (9)
2. Cook food on metal bars (5)
3. Become hard (3)
4. Country whose capital is Canberra (9)
7. A particular ability (5)
9. Item used to catch fish (3)

Across

1. Where you go to get on an aeroplane (7)
5. Female chicken (3)
6. Shine like a star (7)
8. Sugary (5)
9. Place providing higher education (7)
11. Opposite of in (3)
12. Put an idea forward for consideration (7)

Down

1. This follows morning (9)
2. A tree which bears acorns (3)
3. A building in which plays are performed (7)
4. Wrong (9)
7. E.g. beetles and earwigs (7)
10. You walk on this (3)

Sudokus

Help the hornets solve the sudokus. Fill in the blank squares so that numbers 1 to 6 appear once in each row, column and 3 x 2 box. See if you are right by flicking to page 96.

				4	3
		5			1
				6	4
1	6				
6			4		
4	2				

ASIAN GIANT HORNETS are the world's largest hornets, also known as 'killer hornets' or 'murder hornets' – which should give a clue as to how deadly they are! These scary territorial creatures feed on other insects such as honeybees!

HARPY EAGLES' rear claws can be up to 10cm long. That's the same length as a grizzly bear's!

Wordsearches

These killer bees are on the hunt for other deadly creatures. Can you help? Search left to right, up and down to find the animals listed in the boxes below. See if you are right by flicking to page 96.

KILLER BEES have been known to chase threats to their hive as far as 500 m. While one bee's sting is painful but not fatal, being stung by a whole swarm at once would be a big problem!

```
c r q f r i g a t e r v
y m o s q u i t o j s l
q l q d e l w z j e y a
o r e i l v z c i r m m
h g e a g l e a u x h m
p i t o h u i s t a a e
h o r n e t f s x m w r
u k i e l t c o l p k g
s x q i t u j w c o d e
e p s s u w j a r r t i
s m r b r s n r z f p e
j j j a l r r y p a a r
```

cassowary
eagle
frigate
hawk
hornet
lammergeier
mosquito
pitohui

p	h	o	f	g	z	r	b	s	n	o	l
x	v	f	v	o	t	p	e	t	r	e	l
k	a	c	b	e	m	u	l	i	p	f	l
e	m	f	a	l	c	o	n	c	t	t	o
s	p	m	o	s	t	r	i	c	h	r	w
f	i	i	v	p	z	w	w	w	o	j	l
i	r	a	u	r	p	b	a	t	r	t	i
m	e	x	l	n	s	f	s	l	a	j	j
s	b	t	t	w	q	d	p	a	a	v	f
o	a	o	u	s	t	p	u	t	r	k	t
x	t	d	r	n	r	f	o	z	s	l	l
a	j	a	e	q	n	a	k	a	u	t	r

emu
falcon
ostrich
owl
petrel
vampire bat
vulture
wasp

SHRIKES impale their prey on long thorns, which they use as a larder!

Mazes

Avoid the mosquitos by working around
the maze until you reach the exit.
See if you are right by flicking to page 97.

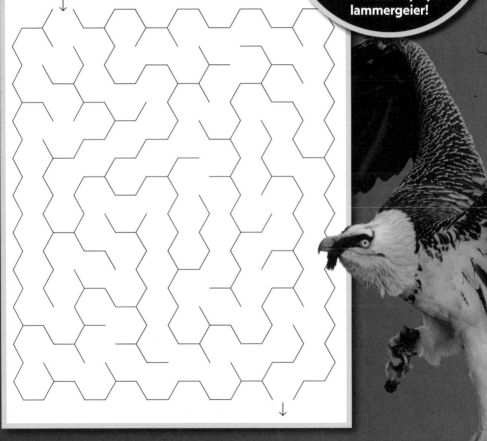

MOSQUITOS are the most deadly insects on the planet because they transmit so many dangerous diseases.

Spot the difference

Compare the cassowary images below.
Can you spot the five differences between the images? See if you are right by flicking to page 97.

See if you are right by flicking to page 97.

CASSOWARIES are flightless, dangerous birds. They have many deadly weapons such as their beaks, powerful legs and dagger-like claws!

Guess what?

1. Cassowaries have developed what to deliver a dangerous kick?
   a. An extra foot
   b. A long, sharp spiked toe
   c. Powerful knees

2. How many species of mosquitoes are there?
   a. Over 3,000
   b. Over 5,000
   c. Over 7,000

3. Carrion, the favourite food of king vultures, is what?
   a. A type of freshwater fish
   b. The decaying flesh of dead animals
   c. The sap of the palm tree

4. Asian giant hornets are also known as:
   a. Goliath hornets
   b. Stinger hornets
   c. Murder hornets

5. Vampire bats are the only mammal to feed entirely on:
   a. Fruit
   b. Insects
   c. Blood

6. Which bird has the largest eye of any land animal?
   a. Ostrich
   b. Bald eagle
   c. Albatross

7. Harpy eagles' rear claws can measure up to:
   a. 3 cm
   b. 10 cm
   c. 18 cm

8. Where can you find a pitohui bird?
   a. New Guinea
   b. Canada
   c. Portugal

9. Blue mud daubers are the main predator of:
   a. Humans
   b. Black and brown widow spiders
   c. Field mice

10. What percentage of a lammergeiers' diet is made up of bones and bone marrow?
    a. 20%
    b. 80%
    c. 100%

SOUTHERN GIANT PETRELS are large aggressive birds that have been known to attack, drown and eat other sea birds. They sometimes spit a horrible-smelling substance at their predators, leading to their 'stinkpot' nickname!

Can you guess the answers to the deadly air animal questions?
Check your answers by flicking to page 97.

PITOHUIS are the only toxic birds in the world! They may look quite cute, but their feathers contain one of the most deadly toxins known to science! This is because of the small but toxic beetles that these birds eat as part of their diet.

Close-ups

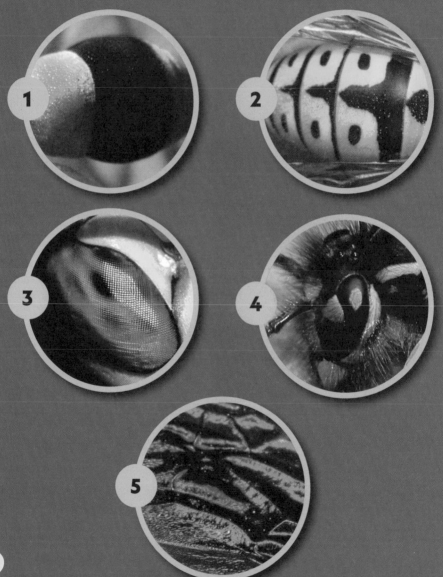

Can you match the wasp close-ups on the left with the pictures below? See if you are right by flicking to page 97.

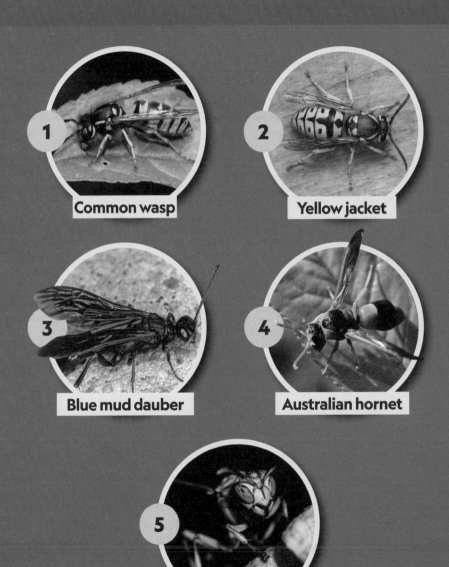

1 Common wasp

2 Yellow jacket

3 Blue mud dauber

4 Australian hornet

5 Executioner wasp

Word jumbles

Rearrange the jumbled letters to form five of the most dangerous birds in the world. See if you are right by flicking to page 97.

R P A H Y G E E A L

A W S A C S Y R O

T P O I U H I

I K G N
U R L T E U V

S T O H R C I

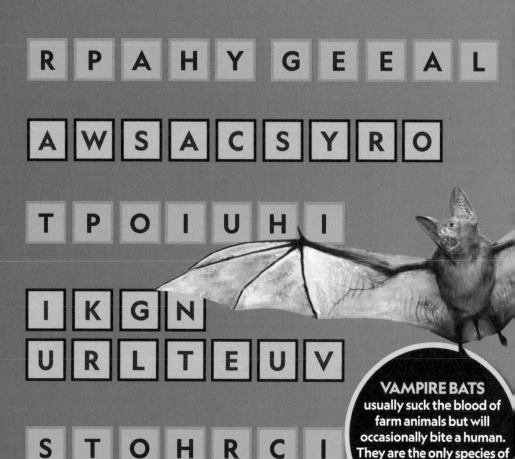

VAMPIRE BATS usually suck the blood of farm animals but will occasionally bite a human. They are the only species of bat that can fly, walk, run and jump!

Word wheels

Can you spell the names of deadly winged creatures using all of the letters in each word wheel?
See if you are right by flicking to page 97.

TSETSE FLIES are large biting flies that carry the African sleeping sickness – a disease which can be deadly if left untreated.

IN THE JUNGLE

Down in the jungle where nobody goes... there are lots of puzzles and facts about deadly animals just waiting to be discovered!

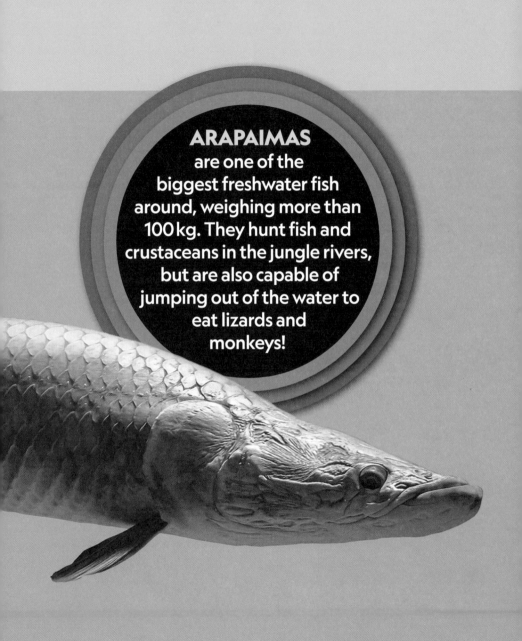

ARAPAIMAS
are one of the
biggest freshwater fish
around, weighing more than
100 kg. They hunt fish and
crustaceans in the jungle rivers,
but are also capable of
jumping out of the water to
eat lizards and
monkeys!

Crosswords

Help the jungle animals crack the crosswords by solving the clues below. Answers have the same amount of letters as the number in brackets. Can you work out the name of the jungle creatures by using the letters in the shaded squares? See if you are right by flicking to page 98.

ASSASSIN BUGS inject their prey with a substance that dissolves their tissues before sucking them up.

Across
- 4   Small (6)
- 6   Seven plus two (4)
- 7   Hired form of transport (4)
- 8   A direction you have to follow (4)
- 9   Part of the mouth around a tooth (3)
- 10 Opposite of pull (4)
- 11 Bird with a big and brightly coloured beak (6)

Down
- 1   Your way of writing your name (9)
- 2   Without a curve; direct (8)
- 3   Polite name for a male (9)
- 5   Huge (8)

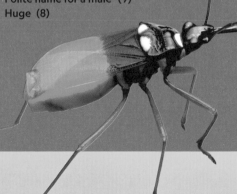

BLACK CAIMAN can be as long as 5 m and will eat pretty much anything that is unlucky enough to come near them.

Across
1 Underground passage through which traffic passes (6)
6 Very good (9)
7 Vend (4)
8 Leg joint (4)
9 Approve or suggest someone or something (9)
11 Very unpleasant (6)

Down
1 Precious gems and other valuable items (8)
2 Jewellery item (8)
3 Slippery snake-like fish (3)
4 Animals that pull Santa's sleigh (8)
5 Was present at (8)
10 Sound a cow makes (3)

Sudokus

Help the spider solve the sudokus.
Fill in the blank squares so
that numbers 1 to 6 appear
once in each row, column
and 3 x 2 box.
See if you are right by
flicking to page 98.

BRAZILIAN WANDERING SPIDERS are recognised as the most dangerous spiders in the world. They defend themselves aggressively and bite if provoked. They prefer to wander along the jungle floor instead of making a web.

			1		6
	4				3
			5	6	
	1	6			
1				2	
3		4			

Puzzle 1 (6×6):

1			3		
	4	3	6		
				2	
	5				
		6	4	1	
		4			6

Puzzle 2 (6×6):

		2		1	
	1		6		
		6		5	
	5		2		
		5		2	
	3		1		

Wordsearches

This electric eel is on hunt for other deadly creatures. Can you help? Search left to right, up and down to find the dealdly words listed in the boxes below. See if you are right by flicking to page 98.

anaconda
bullet ant
dart frog
jaguar

piranha
puma
sting
venom

k	e	e	e	f	v	a	l	l	o	r	n
p	w	s	b	r	s	r	w	j	i	l	u
i	s	r	u	r	j	a	g	u	a	r	x
s	t	u	l	u	e	e	h	r	o	d	t
z	i	r	l	r	c	y	l	p	j	a	q
l	n	r	e	o	v	p	u	m	a	r	a
l	g	d	t	f	e	z	l	x	k	t	s
r	h	j	a	t	n	t	u	o	j	f	i
g	u	i	n	v	o	l	z	l	u	r	y
i	y	w	t	u	m	t	d	r	r	o	v
r	a	n	a	c	o	n	d	a	p	g	b
h	s	p	i	r	a	n	h	a	d	b	a

ELECTRIC EELS are not actually eels, they are a type of knifefish that can generate an electric shock as strong as 600 volts!

GIANT CENTIPEDES can grow to be 30 cm long. The have clawed 'forcipules' that inject powerful venom.

arapaima
assassin bug
black caiman
boa
centipede
electric eel
poison
predator

t	p	r	t	a	h	c	e	e	w	a	e
a	r	a	p	a	i	m	a	u	r	s	l
c	u	y	o	t	a	p	p	s	b	s	e
r	w	p	i	e	t	w	c	m	p	a	c
r	m	m	s	u	e	i	e	f	r	s	t
t	w	c	o	p	n	t	n	e	e	s	r
s	l	d	n	l	e	u	t	i	d	i	i
b	l	a	c	k	c	a	i	m	a	n	c
r	b	o	a	o	y	s	p	y	t	b	e
v	a	t	s	t	v	y	e	o	o	u	e
r	p	j	a	u	m	z	d	e	r	g	l
t	a	x	b	d	n	p	e	l	s	f	o

Mazes

Escape the jaguar by working around the maze until you reach the exit. See if you are right by flicking to page 99.

JAGUARS hunt during the day and at night. Prey includes capybaras, iguanas, tapirs and a whole lot more!

THE GREEN ANACONDA is the heaviest snake in the world and can weigh over 200 kg!

Spot the difference

Compare the jaguar images below.
Can you spot the five differences between the images?
See if you are right by flicking to page 99.

See if you are right by flicking to page 99.

JAGUARS
have the most
powerful bite of all
big cats relative
to their size.

Guess what?

1. **How fast can a puma run?**
   a. 25 km/h
   b. 75 km/h
   c. 120 km/h

2. **The shock of an electric eel has been known to knock what off its feet?**
   a. A horse
   b. An elephant
   c. A moose

3. **What is the heaviest snake species?**
   a. Boa constrictor
   b. Amethystine python
   c. Green anaconda

4. **Which cat has the most powerful bite, relative to its size?**
   a. Tiger
   b. Lynx
   c. Jaguar

5. **Brazilian wandering spiders do what when defending themselves?**
   a. Lift their body up on their hind legs
   b. Spit venom
   c. Change colour

6. **Arapaimas can survive up to how long out of the water?**
   a. 2 hours
   b. 16 hours
   c. 24 hours

7. **Black caimans can be as long as?**
   a. 5 m
   b. 10 m
   c. 12 m

8. **Which insect has the most painful sting?**
   a. Bumblebee
   b. Bullet ant
   c. Horsefly

9. **Poison dart frogs show they are toxic by?**
   a. Being brightly coloured
   b. Screaming loudly
   c. Secreting mucus

10. **Giant centipedes can grow to be how long?**
    a. 10 cm
    b. 30 cm
    c. 50 cm

PAYARAS are large fish with even larger teeth. They use their massive fangs to impale other fish so they can't get away!

Can you guess the answers to the deadly jungle animal questions? Check your answers by flicking to page 99.

POISON DART FROGS are some of the most poisonous animals in the jungle.

GOLDEN POISON FROGS can be yellow, orange or green. They are brightly coloured to warn potential predators of their toxicity.

Word wheels

Can you spell the names of deadly jungle animals using all of the letters in each word wheel? See if you are right by flicking to page 99.

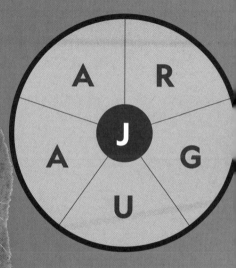

A R J A G U

PUMAS are amazingly agile and can jump as high as 4.6 m!

I A
N **A** R
P H

F O
R **R** T
G A
D

RED-BELLIED PIRANHAS are ferocious predators that may go into a feeding frenzy when hungry.

OVER THE SAVANNA

Let's venture into the world's grasslands with some wild facts and savanna animal puzzles!

HYENAS have one of the most powerful bites among mammals! They can deliver a biting force which is even stronger than tigers and lions!

Crosswords

Help the savanna animals crack the crosswords by solving the clues below. Answers have the same amount of letters as the number in brackets. Can you work out the names of the savanna creatures using the letters in the shaded squares? See if you are right by flicking to page 100.

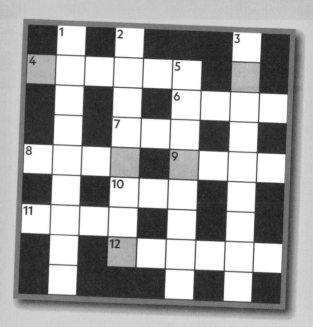

Across

4 Truthful (6)
6 Compass point (4)
7 Frozen form of water (3)
8 Thought or suggestion (4)
9 Require (4)
10 Noise made by sheep (3)
11 Telephone (4)
12 Number in a football team (6)

Down

1 E.g. Monopoly or Cluedo (5,4)
2 Trustworthy (8)
3 Unexplained things (9)
5 Person aged 13-19 (8)

BLACK MAMBAS are considered some of the most deadly snakes on the planet because they're so fast and so venomous! Just two drops of its venom is enough to kill a person.

BLACK RHINOCEROS are most deadly to other black rhinoceros. Fights between each other often end in death.

Across

4 Green vegetables (9)
6 Spider's trap (3)
8 Building where people live (5)
9 Part of the hand (5)
10 Lower and raise your head as a way of saying yes (3)
12 Practice session (9)

Down

1 Make better (4)
2 Creature like a frog or toad (9)
3 Go back (6)
5 The rate at which something moves (5)
6 What the seas are filled with (5)
7 Purchased (6)
11 Egg-shaped (4)

Sudokus

Help the baboons solve the sudokus. Fill in the blank squares so that numbers 1 to 6 appear once in each row, column and 3 x 2 box. See if you are right by flicking to page 100.

	3				1
4	1				
					3
6					
				5	4
1				6	

BABOONS can be ferocious killers and have been known to kill lion cubs if they find them unattended by adult lions!

Top puzzle

6			5		
3					
2		4			
			6		2
					3
		1			5

Bottom puzzle

2				4	
	5				6
	4	2		6	
	6		4	5	
6				3	
	2				4

Wordsearches

This grizzly bear is on the hunt for other deadly creatures. Can you help? Search left to right, up and down to find the animals listed in the boxes below. See if you are right by flicking to page 100.

- baboon
- black mamba
- black rhino
- hippopotamus
- honey badger
- hyena
- king cobra
- scorpion

b	l	a	c	k	m	a	m	b	a	k	a
l	k	r	q	h	a	u	l	w	g	y	i
h	i	p	p	o	p	o	t	a	m	u	s
s	n	e	a	n	p	u	i	l	l	f	k
c	g	s	x	e	u	r	l	k	j	s	b
o	c	t	t	y	s	r	k	c	h	x	a
r	o	m	r	b	i	a	l	t	m	r	b
p	b	b	l	a	c	k	r	h	i	n	o
i	r	i	y	d	p	n	t	s	z	s	o
o	a	l	z	g	t	c	o	a	f	r	n
n	l	q	c	e	n	o	o	q	y	u	i
r	s	j	r	r	h	y	e	n	a	l	z

GRIZZLY BEARS are dangerous because they can run as fast as 50 km/h and have a bite so strong it could crush a bowling ball!

CAPE BUFFALOS
are also known as 'black death' because they're so dangerous and highly unpredictable. Just look at those horns!

m	l	r	s	o	l	i	o	n	p	a	r
k	o	m	o	d	o	d	r	a	g	o	n
h	n	w	a	l	u	z	s	a	g	o	e
u	s	f	p	t	s	a	g	u	t	t	o
a	q	y	v	t	a	d	f	s	m	q	p
t	p	n	i	y	q	d	c	n	e	p	d
n	f	v	s	g	b	e	o	o	l	t	s
b	o	l	s	m	p	r	y	j	a	r	u
l	w	w	i	l	d	d	o	g	s	k	p
p	o	g	c	k	s	i	t	r	e	s	k
n	l	l	c	e	c	h	e	e	t	a	h
o	f	p	o	y	t	t	i	g	e	r	u

adder
cheetah
coyote
komodo dragon
lion
tiger
wild dog
wolf

Mazes

Avoid the scorpions by scurrying around the maze until you reach the exit.
See if you are right by flicking to page 101.

EMPEROR SCORPIONS are one of the biggest scorpions in the world. They're not considered dangerous to humans, but they do have enormous claws that they use to rip their prey apart, which is terrifying enough!

HIPPOPOTAMUS are considered one of the most dangerous large animals around. Their jaws are so powerful that they can break a canoe in half with one bite.

Spot the difference

Compare the hippopotamus images blelow.
Can you spot the five differences between the images?

See if you are right by flicking to page 101.

HIPPOS
are the heaviest
land animal after
elephants.

Guess what?

1. **Vice-grip jaws and specialised teeth help hyenas do what?**
   a. Play fetch
   b. Slice through thick skin and meat
   c. Climb up trees

2. **How fast can a black mamba move?**
   a. 19 km/h
   b. 39 km/h
   c. 59 km/h

3. **How much do baboons weigh?**
   a. Up to 37 kg
   b. Up to 137 kg
   c. Up to 237 kg

4. **Grizzly bear claws are how long?**
   a. 1 cm
   b. 10 cm
   c. 50 cm

5. **Which continent are hippopotamuses native to?**
   a. Europe
   b. Asia
   c. Africa

6. **The king cobra can produce enough neurotoxin in a single bite to kill:**
   a. 10 people
   b. 20 people
   c. 30 people

7. **What is a group of lions called?**
   a. Pride
   b. Herd
   c. School

8. **Which is the largest species of lizard alive?**
   a. Iguana
   b. Gecko
   c. Komodo dragon

9. **Adult emperor scorpions use what to catch their prey:**
   a. Silk webs
   b. Strong pincers
   c. Booby traps

10. **Spitting cobras aim their venom at their prey's:**
    a. Eyes
    b. Mouth
    c. Stomach

HONEY BADGERS have a reputation for being fearless. They have a powerful bite and a thick hide as well as a massive attitude problem! Honey badgers are always up for a fight and are rarely known to back down from a challenge.

Can you guess the answers to the deadly
savanna animal questions?
Check your guesses by flicking to page 101.

KING COBRAS are incredibly fast and venomous. They are the longest venomous snake in the world and one bite contains enough venom to kill 20 humans or one elephant!

Word jumbles

Rearrange the jumbled letters to form five deadly kinds of snake you might find lurking in the grasslands. See if you are right by sss-slithering to page 101.

G K N I   R A C B O

F P F U   D A D R E

K B A L C   A B M M A

KOMODO DRAGONS are the heaviest lizards in the world. They have razor-sharp teeth and a venom that causes their prey to keep bleeding from their wounds and weaken more quickly.

LIONS tend to hunt in packs because their prey is often very fast – they have to use tactics and work together to earn their meals!

R P E I A I R

T E L R A S T E K N A

L B L U K A S E N

73

Word wheels

Can you spell the names of deadly savanna animals using all of the letters in each word wheel? See if you are right by flicking to page 101.

PUFF ADDERS are venomous vipers with an aggressive disposition. When in danger, these snakes 'puff up' in size, hence their name.

NILE CROCODILES live in the African savanna. They eat mainly fish, however, this ferocious predator is known to attack and feed on larger animals such as zebra and wildebeest.

ACROSS THE DESERT

Beware! We're about to cross the desert, where many more dangerous facts and deadly puzzles are watching and waiting in the sand!

SAW SCALED VIPERS are found in the dry deserts of Africa and Asia. They are small in size but are highly aggressive and possess deadly venom.

Crosswords

DESERT RECLUSE SPIDERS have a very dangerous bite which is necrotic, meaning the skin around the bite dies really quickly!

Help the desert animals crack the crosswords by solving the clues below. Answers have the same amount of letters as the number in brackets. Can you work out the names of the desert creatures using the letters in the shaded squares? See if you are right by flicking to page 102.

Across
1 An idea (7)
6 Extremely precise (5)
7 Person who watches an event (9)
8 E.g. Pacific or Atlantic (5)
9 Far away (7)

Down
1 Device used to study stars and planets (9)
2 Words of welcome (9)
3 A vehicle used on farms (7)
4 Stop the progress of an activity (9)
5 Imaginary (7)

FAT-TAILED SCORPION'S Latin name, 'Androctonus', means 'man killer!

Across
1 Small red fruit (9)
5 How old you are (3)
7 Look after (7)
8 USA (7)
11 Cover; bottle top (3)
12 All people (9)

Down
1 Change the order of items (9)
2 The first part of a staircase (4)
3 Flower given on Valentine's Day (4)
4 The day before today (9)
6 Theme or subject (5)
9 Otherwise (4)
10 Too (4)

Sudokus

Help the viper solve the sudokus.
Fill in the blank squares so that numbers
1 to 6 appear once in each row, column and
3 x 2 box. See if you are right by flicking to
page 102.

		4		5	
		6			4
1				2	
	2				1
5			2		
	4		1		

GILA MONSTERS are one of the few venomous lizards in the world. They have bright orange markings on their body and can lock their jaws once they have bitten into flesh.

HORNED VIPERS
have long, hollow, hinged fangs that rotate and can be folded away. When hunting, these snakes like to ambush their prey.

Wordsearch

This taipan sanke is on the hunt for other deadly creatures. Can you help? Search left to right, up and down to find the animals listed in the box below. See if you are right by flicking to page 102.

INLAND TAIPANS are the most venomous snakes on the planet, with the most toxic venom of any reptile in the world.

gila monster
horned viper
kangaroo
red back
scorpion
taipan
velvet ant
wild boar

w	a	v	e	l	v	e	t	a	n	t	a
s	x	i	w	t	r	k	p	o	v	f	h
a	b	m	i	o	r	a	a	d	o	k	o
t	v	u	l	a	e	n	t	a	u	c	r
n	v	v	d	f	d	g	a	v	z	l	n
o	w	i	b	l	b	a	t	i	a	b	e
v	f	r	o	y	a	r	c	p	t	i	d
r	p	m	a	b	c	o	f	p	q	x	v
p	o	x	r	r	k	o	t	p	q	s	i
g	i	l	a	m	o	n	s	t	e	r	p
q	s	c	o	r	p	i	o	n	a	l	e
t	a	i	p	a	n	d	n	s	n	c	r

Word wheels

Can you spell the names of deadly desert animals using all of the letters in each word wheel? See if you are right by flicking to page 102.

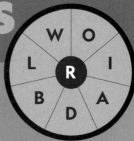

KANGAROOS have an extremely powerful kick that can crush bones!

Mazes

Avoid the spiders by crawling around
the maze until you reach the exit.
See if you are right by flicking to page 103.

**RED-BACK
SPIDERS** are closely
related to black widow
spiders, both of which are
among the most
venomous (and scary-
looking) spiders
around!

VELVET ANTS aren't actually ants. They're a kind of wasp that resembles ants because the females of the species are wingless. Female velvet ants are known as 'cow killers' thanks to their extremely painful sting!

Spot the difference

Compare the gila monster images below.
Can you spot the five differences between the images?
See if you are right by flicking to page 103.

GILA MONSTERS can store fat in their large tails and use it to go for months between meals.

Guess what?

1. How many eyes does a desert recluse spider have?
   a. 2
   b. 6
   c. 10

2. How far can kangaroos leap in a single bound?
   a. 3 m
   b. 5 m
   c. 9 m

3. Horned viper's venom is made up of how many toxins?
   a. 1
   b. 13
   c. 33

4. A group of wild boars is called a?
   a. Sounder
   b. Prickle
   c. Committee

5. What does the tarantula hawk wasp hunt?
   a. Tarantulas
   b. Worms
   c. Ants

6. What are velvet ants also known as?
   a. Lion tamers
   b. Elephant assassins
   c. Cow killers

7. How big can Indian red scorpions grow?
   a. 0.9 cm
   b. 9 cm
   c. 90 cm

8. Which snake is the most venomous?
   a. Inland taipan
   b. King cobra
   c. Rattlesnake

9. Gila monsters can survive on how many big meals a year?
   a. 12
   b. 6
   c. 3

10. Where would you find the redback spider?
    a. North America
    b. Europe
    c. Australia

WESTERN DIAMONDBACK RATTLESNAKES are found in the USA and Mexico. They have heat sensing pits that are used to detect their prey.

Can you guess the answers to the deadly desert animal questions?
Check your answers by flicking to page 103.

TARANTULA HAWKS are wasps with an incredibly powerful sting that injects paralytic venom into tarantulas so that the wasps can lay their eggs in the spider's paralysed body!

Close-ups

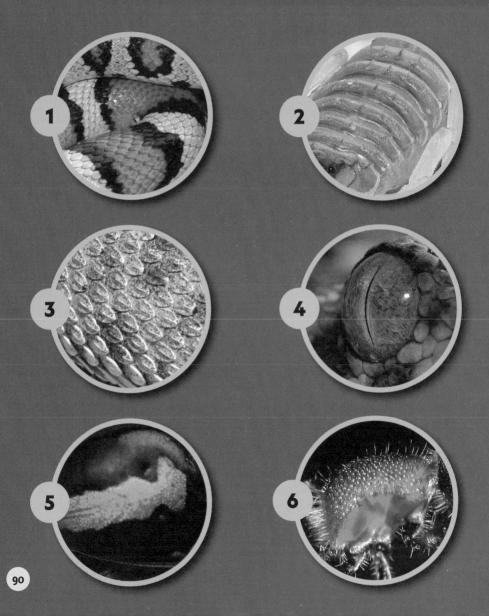

Can you match the deadly desert creature close-ups on the left with the pictures below? See if you are right by flicking to page 103.

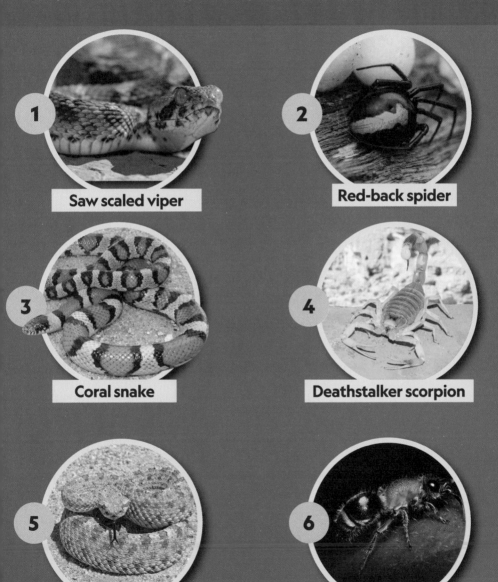

1. Saw scaled viper

2. Red-back spider

3. Coral snake

4. Deathstalker scorpion

5. Sidewinder

6. Velvet ant

Word jumbles

Rearrange the jumbled letters to form five deadly desert animals
See if you are right by slithering to page 103.

V V E L T E
T A N

L A C R O
K S N E A

CORAL SNAKES have a diet that consists of lizards, frogs and small snakes. Sometimes they even eat other coral snakes!

G A L I
R M E N O T S

A W S

C E A L D S

I V R E P

To attract prey, young **SIDEWINDERS** move their tail so it resembles an insect. This deception lures lizards close to the snake making them easier to hunt.

E N O H R D

I R P E V

SOLUTIONS

Pages 8–9

Keyword: JELLYFISH

Keyword: SEA SNAKE

Pages 10–11

6	1	3	4	5	2
4	5	2	1	3	6
3	6	1	2	4	5
5	2	4	6	1	3
1	3	6	5	2	4
2	4	5	3	6	1

4	2	5	6	1	3
6	1	3	5	2	4
3	5	6	2	4	1
1	4	2	3	5	6
5	3	1	4	6	2
2	6	4	1	3	5

5	1	6	4	2	3
3	2	4	5	6	1
1	4	2	3	5	6
6	3	5	2	1	4
4	5	1	6	3	2
2	6	3	1	4	5

Pages 12–13

Pages 14–15

Pages 16–17

Page 18

1. b. 70 years
2. a. 26
3. c. Box jellyfish
4. c. Venomous spines
5. b. Hammerhead shark

6. a. Twilight zone
7. a. Moray eels
8. b. 60 km/h
9. a. Pufferfish
10. b. 120 cm

Pages 20–21

1 – 3   Textile cone snail
2 – 6   Flower urchin
3 – 1   Box Jellyfish

4 – 5   Striped
       sturgeonfish
5 – 4   Lionfish
6 – 2   Stonefish

Page 22

Great white
Sea snake
Pufferfish

Page 23

Viperfish
Stonefish
Barracuda

SOLUTIONS

Pages 26–27

Keyword: VULTURE

Keyword: FRIGATE

Pages 28–29

2	1	6	5	4	3
3	4	5	6	2	1
5	3	2	1	6	4
1	6	4	2	3	5
6	5	3	4	1	2
4	2	1	3	5	6

5	1	2	3	4	6
3	4	6	2	5	1
2	3	5	6	1	4
4	6	1	5	3	2
1	2	3	4	6	5
6	5	4	1	2	3

6	3	1	4	2	5
2	5	4	6	3	1
3	1	5	2	4	6
4	6	2	1	5	3
5	4	6	3	1	2
1	2	3	5	6	4

Pages 30–31

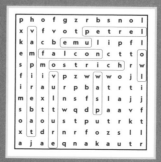

Pages 32–33

Pages 34–35

Page 36

1. b. A long, sharp spiked toe
2. a. Over 3,000
3. b. The decaying flesh of dead animals
4. c. Murder hornets
5. c. Blood
6. a. Ostrich
7. b. 10 cm
8. a. New Guinea
9. b. Black and brown widow spiders
10. b. 80%

Pages 38–39

1 – 4 Australian hornet
2 – 2 Yellow jacket
3 – 5 Executioner wasp
4 – 1 Common wasp
5 – 3 Blue mud dauber

Page 40

Harpy eagle
Cassowary
Pitohuis
King vulture
Ostrich

Page 41

Hornet
Cassowary

SOLUTIONS

Pages 44–45

```
  S S       G
L I T T L E E
  G   R   N I N E
  N   A   O   T
T A X I   R U L E
  T   G U M   E
P U S H O   M
  R   T O U C A N
  E       S   N
```

Keyword: CAIMAN

```
T U N N E L
R   E   E   R   A
E X C E L L E N T
A   K       I   T
S E L L   K N E E
U   A       D   N
R E C O M M E N D
E   E   O   E   E
      H O R R I D
```

Keyword: ANACONDA

Pages 46–47

2	5	3	1	4	6
6	4	1	2	5	3
4	3	2	5	6	1
5	1	6	4	3	2
1	6	5	3	2	4
3	2	4	6	1	5

1	6	5	3	4	2
2	4	3	6	5	1
6	3	1	5	2	4
4	5	2	1	6	3
3	2	6	4	1	5
5	1	4	2	3	6

6	4	2	5	1	3
5	1	3	6	4	2
3	2	6	4	5	1
4	5	1	2	3	6
1	6	5	3	2	4
2	3	4	1	6	5

Pages 48–49

Pages 50–51

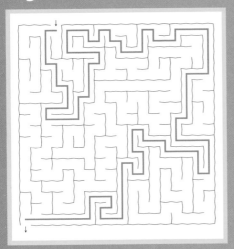

Pages 52–53

Page 54

1. b. 75 km/h
2. a. A horse
3. c. Green anaconda
4. c. Jaguar
5. a. Lift their body up on their hind legs
6. c. 24 hours
7. a. 5 m
8. b. Bullet ant
9. a. Being brightly coloured
10. b. 30 cm

Page 56–57

Jaguar
Piranha
Dart frog

SOLUTIONS

Pages 60-61

Keyword: HYENA

Keyword: BABOON

Pages 62-63

2	3	6	5	4	1
4	1	5	2	3	6
5	4	1	6	2	3
6	2	3	4	1	5
3	6	2	1	5	4
1	5	4	3	6	2

6	1	2	5	3	4
3	4	5	1	2	6
2	6	4	3	5	1
1	5	3	6	4	2
5	2	6	4	1	3
4	3	1	2	6	5

2	3	6	5	4	1
4	5	1	3	2	6
5	4	2	1	6	3
1	6	3	4	5	2
6	1	4	2	3	5
3	2	5	6	1	4

Pages 64-65

Pages 66–67

Pages 68–69

Page 70

1. b. Slice through thick skin and meat
2. a. 19 km/h
3. a. 37 kg
4. b. 10 cm
5. c. Africa
6. b. 20 people
7. a. Pride
8. c. Komodo dragon
9. b. Strong pincers
10. a. Eyes

Pages 72–73

King cobra
Puff adder
Black mamba
Prairie rattlesnake
Bull snake

Page 75

King cobra
Cheetah
Hippopotamus

SOLUTIONS

Pages 78–79

T	H	O	U	G	H	T		I	
E			R		R			N	
L		P		E	X	A	C	T	
E		R		E		C		E	
S	P	E	C	T	A	T	O	R	
C		T		I		O		R	
O	C	E	A	N		R		U	
P		N		G				P	
E		D	I	S	T	A	N	T	

Keyword: SCORPION

R	A	S	P	B	E	R	R	Y	
E		T			O			E	
A	G	E		T	S	S		S	
R		P	R	O	T	E	C	T	
R				P				E	
A	M	E	R	I	C	A		R	
N		L		C	L	I	D		
G		S			S		S	A	
E	V	E	R	Y	B	O	D	Y	

Keyword: VIPER

Pages 80–81

3	1	4	6	5	2
2	5	6	3	1	4
1	6	5	4	2	3
4	2	3	5	6	1
5	3	1	2	4	6
6	4	2	1	3	5

4	5	3	6	1	2
1	6	2	5	4	3
2	1	6	4	3	5
3	4	5	1	2	6
5	2	4	3	6	1
6	3	1	2	5	4

4	6	2	5	3	1
1	3	5	2	6	4
2	1	6	3	4	5
3	5	4	1	2	6
5	4	3	6	1	2
6	2	1	4	5	3

Page 82

Page 83

Wild boar
Kangaroo
Taipan

Pages 84-85

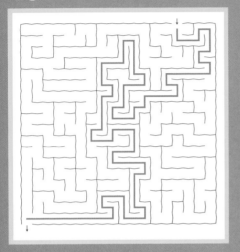

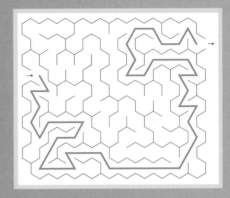

Pages 86-87

Page 88

1. b. 6
2. c. 9 m
3. b. 13
4. a. Sounder
5. a. Tarantulas
6. c. Cow killers
7. b. 9 cm
8. a. Inland taipan
9. c. 3
10. c. Australia

Pages 90-91

1-3 Coral snake
2-4 Deathstalker scorpion
3-5 Sidewinder
4-1 Saw scaled viper
5-2 Red-back spider
6-6 Velvet ant

Pages 92-93

Velvet ant
Coral snake
Gila monster
Saw scaled viper
Horned viper

Look for more puzzle books in this series!